SRA

Early Interventions in Reading

Challenge Stories

Columbus, OH

The McGraw-Hill Companies

MHEonline.com

Imprint 2012

Send all inquiries to:
SRA/McGraw-Hill
8787 Orion Place
Columbus, OH 43240

Printed in the United States of America.

ISBN 0-07-602667-1

11 12 QVS 16 15 14

Table of Contents

About the Challenge Stories

The ***SRA Early Interventions in Reading*** *Challenge Stories* allow your students to apply their knowledge of phonic elements to read simple, engaging texts. Each story supports instruction in a new phonic element and incorporates elements and words that have been learned earlier.

The students can fold and staple the pages of each challenge story to make books of their own to keep and read. We suggest that you keep extra sets of the stories in your classroom for the children to reread.

How to fold a challenge story

1. Tear out the pages you need.

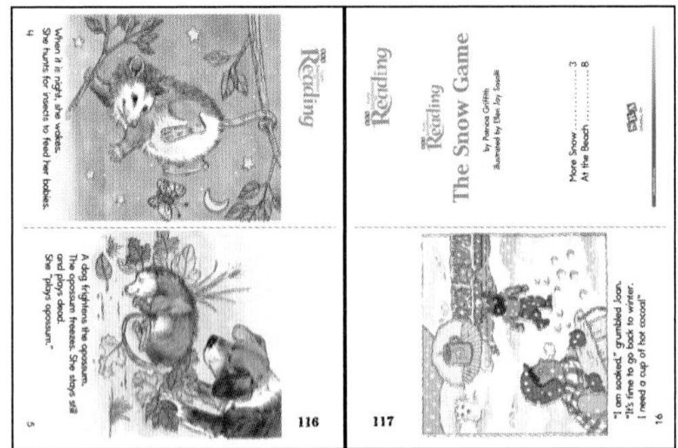

2. For 16-page stories, place pages 8 and 9, 6 and 11, 4 and 13, and 2 and 15 faceup.

2. For 8-page stories, place pages 4 and 5 and pages 2 and 7 faceup.

For 16-page book

3. Place the pages on top of each other in this order: pages 8 and 9, pages 6 and 11, pages 4 and 13, and pages 2 and 15.

4. Fold along the center line.

5. Check to make sure the pages are in order.

6. Staple the pages along the fold.

For 8-page book

3. Place pages 4 and 5 on top of pages 2 and 7.

4. Fold along the center line.

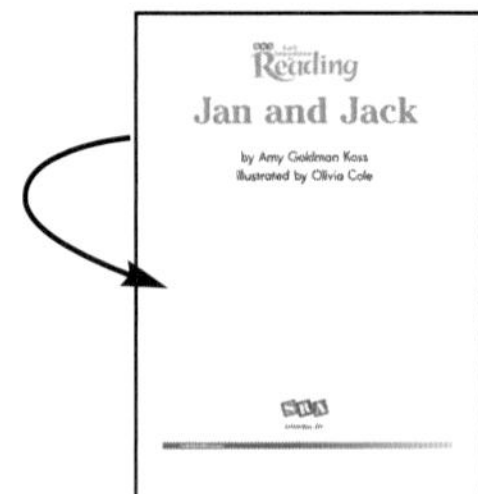

5. Check to make sure the pages are in order.

6. Staple the pages along the fold.

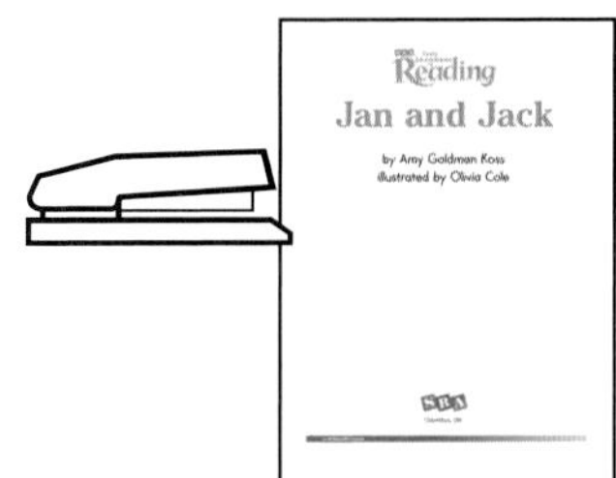

Just to let you know...

A message from ______________________________

Help your child discover the joy of independent reading with ***SRA Early Interventions in Reading.*** From time to time your child will bring home his or her very own challenge story to share with you. With your help, these stories can give your child important reading practice and a joyful shared reading experience.

You may want to set aside a few minutes every evening to read these stories together. Here are some suggestions you may find helpful:

- Do not expect your child to read each story perfectly, but concentrate on sharing the book together.
- Participate by doing some of the reading.
- Talk about the stories as you read, give lots of encouragement, and watch as your child becomes more fluent throughout the year!

Learning to read takes lots of practice. Sharing these stories is one way that your child can gain that valuable practice. Encourage your child to keep the challenge stories in a special place. This collection will make a library of books that your child can read and reread. Take the time to listen to your child read from his or her library. Just a few moments of shared reading each day can give your child the confidence needed to excel in reading.

Children who read every day come to think of reading as a pleasant, natural part of life. One way to inspire your child to read is to show that reading is an important part of your life by letting him or her see you reading books, magazines, newspapers, or any other materials. Another good way to show that you value reading is to share a challenge story with your child each day.

Successful reading experiences allow children to be proud of their newfound reading ability. Support your child with interest and enthusiasm about reading. You won't regret it!

Para su conocimiento...

Un mensaje de ______________________________

Ayude a su niño o niña a descubrir el placer de la lectura individual con ***SRA Early Interventions in Reading.*** De vez en cuando, su niño(a) llevará a casa su propio cuento para practicar para compartirlo con usted. Con su ayuda, estos cuentos pueden constituir un ejercicio importante para mejorar la lectura y una experiencia placentera de lectura compartida.

Disponga de unos minutos en las noches para leer estos cuentos con su niño(a). Estas sugerencias lo pueden ayudar:

- No espere que lea el cuento a la perfección, concéntrese sólo en leer el libro juntos.
- Participe leyendo fragmentos del cuento.
- Conforme lean, comente con su niño(a) los cuentos, aliéntelo constantemente y observe cómo mejora su fluidez durante el año.

Aprender a leer requiere mucha práctica. Compartir estos cuentos es una forma de ayudar a su niño(a) a adquirir esa valiosa destreza. Anímelo a guardar los cuentos para practicar en un lugar especial. Esta colección constituirá una biblioteca que el niño podrá leer y releer. Dedique tiempo a escuchar a su niño(a) cuando lea los libros de su biblioteca. Tan sólo unos momentos de lectura compartida todos los días le darán a su niño(a) la confianza necesaria para convertirse en un excelente lector.

Los niños que leen todos los días llegan a hacer de la lectura una parte placentera y natural de la vida. Una forma de inspirar a su niño(a) a leer es demonstrarle que la lectura es un aspecto importante para usted; propicie que lo vea leer libros, revistas, periódicos y otras publicaciones. Otra buena manera de demostrarle que usted valora la lectura es compartiendo con él(ella) un cuento para practicar todos los días.

Las experiencias exitosas con la lectura hacen que los niños se sientan orgullosos de su recién adquirida habilidad para leer. Apoye a su niño(a) demostrando interés y entusiasmo en la lectura. ¡No se arrepentirá!

Pat and Pam snap up Tim's ham and mints.
Pat and Pam: Mmmm! Ham and mints!

SRA Early Interventions in Reading

Pat and Pam

by Aleta Naylor
illustrated by Len Epstein

Columbus, OH

The McGraw-Hill Companies

SRAonline.com

SRA

Printed in the United States of America.

Send all inquiries to:
SRA/McGraw-Hill
8787 Orion Place
Columbus, OH 43240-4027

The McGraw-Hill Companies

2

Pam: Tim naps! Tim has mints in his hand!

Pat: Look at his pants . . . it is ham!

Pat: Ants can't tip a tin pan.

Tim's Map

Pat taps Pam.

Pat: It is Tim's map.
Pam: It has hints on it.

Pam: And tip Tim's tin pan of mints.

Pat: Pam, spin the tan mat and hop on Tim's ham!

Pat: Tim's map has a ham on it.
Pam: It has mints in a pan.

Pam: Ants like ham and mints.

Pam: Tim's ham is by a tan mat.

Ham and Mints

Pam: It is ham!
Pat: It is mints!

Pat: Let's get Tim, his ham,
and his mints.

Pat tips his hat at the cat as it naps.

Tim's map takes Pat and Pam to Tim's ham and mints.

12

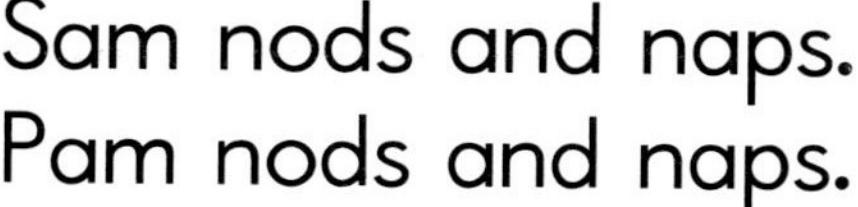

Sam nods and naps.
Pam nods and naps.

Can you help Sam?

11

Grandma Dot tells Pam that Sam is not sad and mad. Babies sob. It is not bad.

Baby Sam

Sam is Pam's baby brother.

SRAonline.com

SRA

Printed in the United States of America.

Send all inquiries to:
SRA/McGraw-Hill
8787 Orion Place
Columbus, OH 43240-4027

The McGraw-Hill Companies

10

Sam is not sad and mad.
Pam is not sad and mad.
Sam nods, and Mom pats him.
Mom and Dad pat Pam.

Pam sits with Sam.
Everyone loves Sam and Pam.

SRA Early Interventions in Reading

Everyone Loves Pam and Sam

by Aleta Naylor
illustrated by Kersti Frigell

Columbus, OH

The McGraw·Hill Companies

13

Pam stops Grandma Dot
and Grandpa Stan.

Sam holds Mom's hand.
Pam holds Dad's hand.

Mom pats and taps Sam.
Pam pats and taps Mom.

Pam stands and says, “Dad.”
Dad cannot help.

Pam stops and taps Mom.
Mom cannot help.

Sam sits with Dad and sips.
Pam sits and sips.

Pam sits and is sad.

16

Pam and Sam

Sam is sad and sobs.
Can someone help?

The vet helped Scat and Sam get well. Sal can have fun with her cats!

SRA Early Interventions in Reading

At the Vet

by Linda Taylor
illustrated by Meryl Henderson

Columbus, OH

The McGraw-Hill Companies

SRAonline.com

SRA

Printed in the United States of America.

Send all inquiries to:
SRA/McGraw-Hill
8787 Orion Place
Columbus, OH 43240-4027

The McGraw-Hill Companies

Sal is glad.
The vet says Scat and Sam will get well.

The vet says the cats are sick.
She says, "The cats got into a bad plant."
The cats get big red pills.

Sal has pet cats.
Sam is a black cat.
Scat is a tan cat.

Scat and Sam are sick.
Sal must take her cats to a vet.
Sal tells her cats, "I will put on a red shirt.
Then we will get in the car."

The cats are in Sal's car.
Scat is glad to get to the vet.
Sam is not glad at the vet.
He will sit in the back of Sal's car.

The fish did not think Fang was bad! In fact, Fang was fun and charming.

SRA Early Interventions in Reading

Fang's Wish

by Elizabeth Falat
illustrated by Len Epstein

Columbus, OH

The McGraw-Hill Companies

SRAonline.com

 SRA

Printed in the United States of America.

Send all inquiries to:
SRA/McGraw-Hill
8787 Orion Place
Columbus, OH 43240-4027

The McGraw-Hill Companies

Fang and the little fish swam.
Then lots of fish swam up to sing and play.
Fang felt glad. Fang had his wish!

"That fin is funny!" the little fish chuckled. "Can I hang on and swim with you?"

Fang Talks with Splash

Fang swam, sang, and played.

But fish did not swim with Fang. Fish did not sing with Fang. Fish did not play with Fang. Fang felt sad.

Then a bunch of fish swam next to Fang and checked Fang's fin. One little fish stopped swimming.

Splash saw Fang.
"Fang, you are a grand shark!" sang Splash.
"I am?" asked Fang.

"Fish will not swim with me," said Fang.

Splash said, “Big fish tell little fish not to swim with sharks. Big fish tell little fish that sharks are bad.”

“Big fish tell little fish that?”
asked Fang.

Splash hung red string on Fang.
“Yes, yes!” said Fang.

Splash pressed sand on the shells. “Yes, yes!” said Fang.

“Big and little fish think sharks are bad.”

“But that’s sad and bad!” grumbled Fang. “Fish can’t **know** me if they can’t swim and sing with me. I am not bad. I think I’m fun and charming.”

"I can help with this problem," said Splash. "I'll get things and swim back fast."

Splash's Plan

Splash swam back with lots of shells. He hung them on Fang's fin.

"Yes, yes!" said Fang. "But do not quit yet!"

Matt was at the vet with Dad.
Frank has found his pal, Matt!

SRA Early Interventions in Reading

Where Is Matt?

by Kristen Salvatore
illustrated by Gary Undercuffler

Columbus, OH

The McGraw-Hill Companies

SRAonline.com

SRA

Printed in the United States of America.

Send all inquiries to:
SRA/McGraw-Hill
8787 Orion Place
Columbus, OH 43240-4027

The McGraw-Hill Companies

It is six o'clock, and there is Dad.
Matt is with Dad!

It says on Dad's note,
"I went to the vet."
Did Matt go with Dad?

Where Is Matt?

Frank has fun with his pal, Matt.
But Frank cannot find Matt.
Where is Matt?

Is Matt in Mom's large car?

What is this?
Dad left a note.

33

No, he is not in Mom's car.

Is Matt hidden in the bed?

What is on this desk?
It's a note.
It's a note from Dad.

A Hint

No Matt in Mom's car or in the bed.
He looked in the kitchen.
Where is Matt?

No, he is not hidden in the bed.

Is Matt fixing tuna and gingersnaps?

No, he is not fixing tuna and gingersnaps.

37

Rick: Pam, we are stuck in mud. Stop and help us. Grab rugs, mats, or socks. But do not pick up rocks or sticks!

SRA Early Interventions in Reading

Stuck!

by Lisa Trumbauer
illustrated by Len Epstein

Columbus, OH

The McGraw-Hill Companies

SRAonline.com

SRA

Printed in the United States of America.

Send all inquiries to:
SRA/McGraw-Hill
8787 Orion Place
Columbus, OH 43240-4027

The McGraw-Hill Companies

Rob Rabbit trips! Bob Bug, Don Duck, Rob Rabbit, and Rick are all stuck back in mud.

Rick: Rob Rabbit, tug Don Duck.
Don Duck, tug Bob Bug.
Bob Bug, tug on my hand.

Stuck in Mud

Bob Bug is stuck.
Bob Bug is stuck in mud.

40

Don Duck is stuck.
Don Duck is stuck in mud.
Don Duck and Bob Bug are stuck in mud.

Rob Rabbit: Don Duck, grab Bob Bug.
Bob Bug, grab Rick's hand.

Rob Rabbit: His stick is stuck in mud!
Don Duck: Bob Bug, tug on
Rick's hand.

Rob Rabbit is stuck in mud.
Rob Rabbit is stuck with Don Duck
and Bob Bug.

Rick sees Bob Bug, Don Duck, and Rob Rabbit stuck in mud.

Rick

Bob Bug, Don Duck, and Rob Rabbit: Rick is stuck in mud! Let's get his big stick.

43

Bob Bug pops up. Don Duck runs up.
Rob Rabbit hops up.
Rick dips back in the mud.

Rick: Bob Bug, hop up on a rock!
Rob Rabbit, run and grab a rock!
Bob Bug: Don Duck is still stuck in mud.

Rob Rabbit: Let's get Don Duck.
Rick: Bob Bug, Don Duck, and Rob Rabbit are stuck back in mud.

Bob Bug: Rick, pick up a big stick.
Rick: Grab on the stick.
Don Duck: Rick, tug the stick!

Chirp felt bad that Scat was locked in the backyard.
He missed that impish little cat.
Chirp sits with his best pal, Scat.

SRA Early Interventions in Reading

Chirp and Scat

by Tony Gates
illustrated by Len Epstein

Columbus, OH

The McGraw-Hill Companies

SRAonline.com

SRA

Printed in the United States of America.

Send all inquiries to:
SRA/McGraw-Hill
8787 Orion Place
Columbus, OH 43240-4027

The McGraw-Hill Companies

Rob hollered at Scat for picking at Barb's spot.
Scat sat puzzled.
Rob locked Scat in the backyard.

47

Chirp had a plan.
Chirp went to Barb's spot and picked at it.

Chirp is a bird.
Scat is a cat.
Chirp and Scat are with Rob and Barb Platt.

Scat was such an impish little cat.
Rob and Barb said, “He is Scat.”

Rob and Barb could not tell that Chirp and Scat were not pals.

“Zack, you napped all night!”

Early Interventions in Reading

Zack’s Nap

by Kristen Salvatore
illustrated by Gary Undercuffler

Columbus, OH

The McGraw-Hill Companies

SRAonline.com

SRA

Printed in the United States of America.

Send all inquiries to:
SRA/McGraw-Hill
8787 Orion Place
Columbus, OH 43240-4027

The McGraw-Hill Companies

At last Zack gets off his bed.
"Mom, didn't I just nap a bit?"

Zack did not get up from his bed.

Time for Bed

Zack's mom says, "It's past time for bed. Let's turn off the TV."
Zack did not.

"But, Mom," grumbles Zack,
"this act has not ended."

"Mom, can I rest a bit?
Didn't I just hop into bed?"

"It's time to get up, Zack.
Get scrubbed and dressed!"

Zack stands up, and his mom
sends him to his bed.

Zack stands at his sink. "Mom, I'm not sleepy. Can I watch TV?"

Time to Wake Up

"Zack, it is past six. The sun is up."

"Mom, don't click off the lamp.
Let me read."

Zack's mom hands him a soap bar.
"It bubbles and suds as you scrub.
It is fun."

Zack stops as he passes the TV.
"There is a big net if she slips."

Zack sits up in his bed. His mom
gets a blanket for Zack's bed.

Big Bill and Little Bill sit on a mat.
Big Bill is not too big, and Little Bill is not too little.
Big Bill and Little Bill are still best friends.

SRA Early Interventions in Reading

Big Bill and Little Bill

by Aleta Naylor
illustrated by Len Epstein

Columbus, OH
The McGraw-Hill Companies

SRAonline.com

SRA

Printed in the United States of America.

Send all inquiries to:
SRA/McGraw-Hill
8787 Orion Place
Columbus, OH 43240-4027

The McGraw-Hill Companies

What can Big Bill and Little Bill do? Where can they sit and snack, nap, and hop?

Big Bill and Little Bill hop on the bed.
But Big Bill is too big.
Big Bill hops and bumps.

Little Bill in a Big House

Big Bill and Little Bill are best friends.
Big Bill asks Little Bill to play.

Big Bill and Little Bill sit.
But Little Bill is too little.
Little Bill slips off.

Big Bill and Little Bill nap.
But Big Bill is too big.
Big Bill falls off the edge.

Big Bill and Little Bill snack.
But Big Bill is too big.
Big Bill flips his fudge.

Big Bill and Little Bill snack.
But Little Bill is too little.
Little Bill can't hop up.

Big Bill and Little Bill nap.
But Little Bill is too little.
Little Bill flips.

Big Bill and Little Bill sit.
But Big Bill is too big.
Big Bill cracks the back.

Big Bill in a Little House

Little Bill and Big Bill are best friends.
Little Bill asks if Big Bill can play.

Big Bill and Little Bill spin fast.
But Little Bill is too little.
Little Bill spins off into the hedge.

What can Little Bill and Big Bill do?
Where can Big Bill and Little Bill sit and snack, nap, and spin?

65

: An octopus! Then you must tell him to keep his hands and arms off my stuff.

SRA Early Interventions in Reading

Pick a Pet

by Meg Michael
illustrated by Susanne DeMarco

Columbus, OH

The McGraw-Hill Companies

SRAonline.com

SRA

Printed in the United States of America.

Send all inquiries to:
SRA/McGraw-Hill
8787 Orion Place
Columbus, OH 43240-4027

The McGraw-Hill Companies

: I will pick an octopus.
An octopus will fetch and whirl.

67

: Then what pet will you pick?

Pets to Pick

: I will pick a pet.

: Do you want birds?

: No, not birds. Birds shed feathers.

: Panthers are not good pets. I will not pick birds or turtles or fish. I will not pick chimps or caterpillars or panthers.

: Then will you pick panthers?
Panthers are big black cats.

: Then do you wish for turtles?
Turtles can swim.

: Not turtles.

: You do not wish for birds or turtles.
Will you pick fish?

: Caterpillars will not do.
I will not pick birds or turtles
or fish or chimps or caterpillars.

A Pet Is Picked

: Perhaps you will pick caterpillars.
Caterpillars will turn into moths.

: I will not pick fish
or birds or turtles.

: Perhaps you will pick chimps.
Chimps are fun.

: I will not pick chimps!
I will not pick birds or turtles
or fish or chimps.

Bart and Meg could see that the giant is a cart.
"I feel brave," said Bart.
"Me, too," said Meg.
Liz had a smile on her face.

Brave Liz

by Dennis Fertig
illustrated by Kersti Frigell

Columbus, OH

The McGraw·Hill Companies

SRAonline.com

SRA

Printed in the United States of America.

Send all inquiries to:
SRA/McGraw-Hill
8787 Orion Place
Columbus, OH 43240-4027

The McGraw-Hill Companies

"It is not a giant," brave Liz yelled
to Bart and Meg.
"It is a cart."
Rumble. Rumble. Rumble.

The cart wheels went "rumble, rumble, rumble."
The giant's eye is a red bag.

The Giant

In the mist on the hill, there was a rumble.
"What is that?" asked Bart.

In the mist at the farm, there was a rumble.
"What is that?" asked Meg.

Rumble. Rumble. Rumble.
The giant is not a giant!
It is a big pile of bags on a cart.

Liz left the castle.
She ran up the hill.
She could see the giant!

In the mist in the castle garden, there was a rumble.
"What is that?" asked Liz.

Rumble. Rumble. Rumble.
Bart, Meg, and Beth run to the castle.
Are they safe in the castle?

Rumble. Rumble. Rumble.
"No!" called Bart and Meg.
Bart and Meg are not brave.

Rumble. Rumble. Rumble.
"Let's run out of the castle to see the giant," said Liz.
Liz is brave.

Rumble. Rumble. Rumble.
What is that?
"A giant!" yelled Bart.

Rumble. Rumble. Rumble.
A giant! Oh no!
What will happen to Bart, Meg, and Liz?

Liz Is Brave

In the castle, Bart, Meg, and Liz can see the giant's big eye.
Oh no!

Then her mom rushes in
and grins a big grin.
"That was an extra long bath!
You are a big girl, Beth!"

SRA Early Interventions in Reading

A Bath for Beth

by Dina McClellan
illustrated by Jan Pyk

Columbus, OH
The McGraw·Hill Companies

SRAonline.com

SRA

Printed in the United States of America.

Send all inquiries to:
SRA/McGraw-Hill
8787 Orion Place
Columbus, OH 43240-4027

The McGraw-Hill Companies

82

Beth hops into her tub.
Beth scrubs and scrubs.
Then she steps out.
"BETH!" her mom calls.
"I'm finished," Beth says.

Beth puts dishes, cups, wax lips, the sax, and fish on her mat. Beth gets them all picked out as fast as she can!

Beth Has Fun

"Beth, Beth! Get into that bath!"

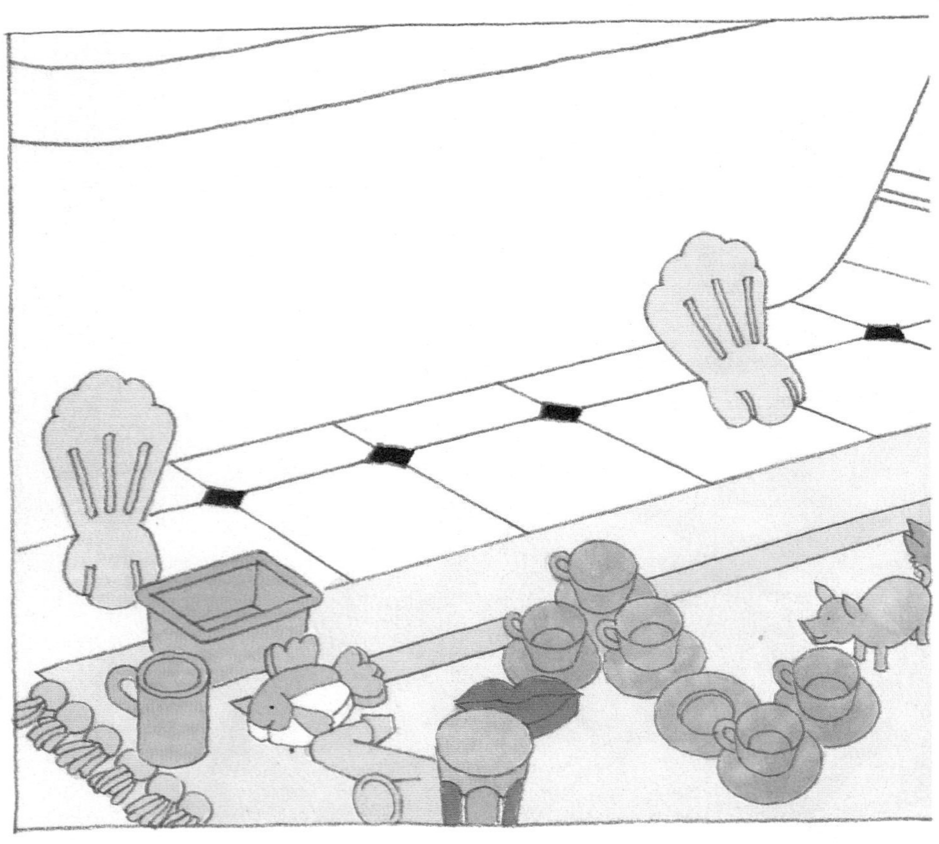

“Yes, Mom,” Beth says,
“after I put all these up.
Then I’ll hop in this tub
and scrub and scrub!”

Beth picks the box,
the fox, pigs, and an ox!

85

Beth Has Her Bath

"BETH, BETH, DID YOU FINISH THAT BATH?"

Water rushes and gushes
from Beth's bath tap.
Bubbles hiss and sizzle and plop.
They fizzle until they pop.

"Beth, Beth! GET INTO THAT BATH!"
On the bath mat is a zigzag path.
Beth sits on that mat and has fun.

Dishes, cups, and fish—
Beth mixes them all up.

Beth drops in fish with fins next.

"Beth, Beth! DID YOU GET INTO THAT BATH?" Beth picks up the box and the little red fox. The box and fox make big splashes as Beth drops them into her bath. Next Beth drops in pigs and an ox.

Beth adds dishes and
cups, for six,

red wax lips, and a sax
to her mix in her bath.

"Jan, I am glad for snacks and a nap."
Jack sits and has his snacks.

Jan and Jack

by Amy Goldman Koss
illustrated by Olivia Cole

Columbus, OH

The McGraw·Hill Companies

SRAonline.com

SRA

Printed in the United States of America.

Send all inquiries to:
SRA/McGraw-Hill
8787 Orion Place
Columbus, OH 43240-4027

The McGraw-Hill Companies

Jan jabs and jiggles Jack.
"Jan, I had to sit and nap," says Jack.

Jack is on the bridge.
Jack naps.

Jan packs Jack's snack.
Jan puts his snack in a jug.

Jan tosses the jug in Jack's backpack.
Jan jogs up hills.
She jogs in grass and mud.

Jan hops a big hedge
and jumps onto a bridge.

Kids can swim in
Quarter Pond too!

SRA Early Interventions in Reading

Quarter Pond

by Stephan Queen
illustrated by Meryl Henderson

Columbus, OH

The McGraw-Hill Companies

SRAonline.com

SRA

Printed in the United States of America

Send all inquiries to:
SRA/McGraw-Hill
8787 Orion Place
Columbus, OH 43240-4027

The McGraw-Hill Companies

Kids squat by Quarter Pond but cannot catch the quick fish.

95

Kids plan a picnic.
Mom puts her quilt
on the grass.

Lots of animals swim
in Quarter Pond.

Squads of ducks quack
and quack.
Ducks do not quit quacking
until dark.

Fish squirt liquid at
bugs to catch them.
This bug is quick,
but this fish is quicker.

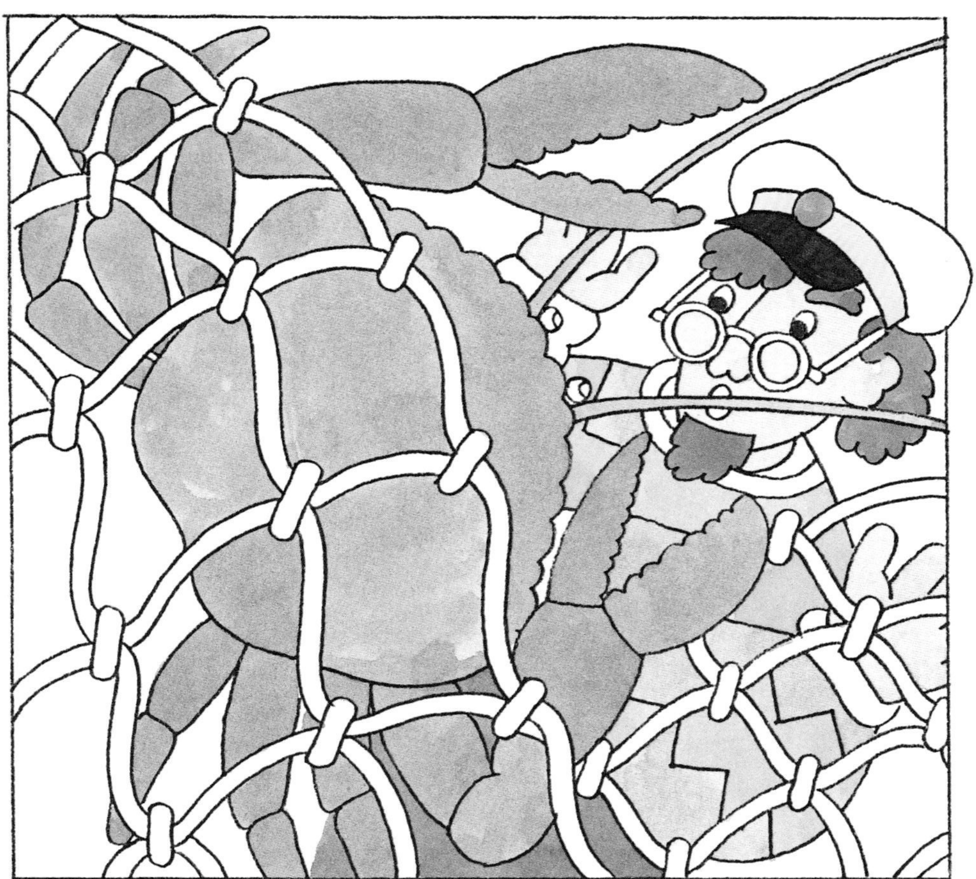

"Perhaps I really don't want crabs at all," said Sailor Paul.

SRA Early Interventions in Reading

Sailor Paul and the Crabs

by Tim Paulson
illustrated by Jan Pyk

Columbus, OH

The McGraw-Hill Companies

SRAonline.com

SRA

Printed in the United States of America.

Send all inquiries to:
SRA/McGraw-Hill
8787 Orion Place
Columbus, OH 43240-4027

The McGraw·Hill Companies

"I'll catch some crabs if it's the last thing I do," said Sailor Paul. When rain began falling, Sailor Paul put an awning on his deck. When a cold wind blew, he put on a shawl. The sea became wild and awful, but Paul would not quit. At last, his nets were full, and Paul began pulling and pulling.

When his nets were full again, Paul quickly pulled them in. “I’m fishing for crabs, not shark!” yelled Sailor Paul. “Get off my deck if you don’t want a fight!” Sailor Paul fished and fished. He netted ten fish, five whales, and a hundred shrimp. But he did not catch one crab.

Sailor Paul liked to catch crabs that walk in the sea. Paul went out in his ship. It was a small fishing boat named Annie. But Paul never caught a single crab.

He set out to sea in the morning. "I'm going to catch a crab today!" yelled Sailor Paul. Later his nets were full, and Paul pulled them up on deck.

"Get away, silly squid," scolded Sailor Paul. "Don't make a mess on my deck. I catch crabs, not squid."

101

Cedric helped Lance and his mom bake apple tarts and bread.
Cedric ate a tart and stopped being bad.

SRA Early Interventions in Reading

Lance's Dragon

by Dina McClellan
illustrated by Len Epstein

Columbus, OH

The McGraw-Hill Companies

SRAonline.com

SRA

Printed in the United States of America.

Send all inquiries to:
SRA/McGraw-Hill
8787 Orion Place
Columbus, OH 43240-4027

The McGraw-Hill Companies

Then Cedric felt bad.
"I will give back the scarf and the bracelet," Cedric said.

103

But Lance was brave.
He grabbed the lace scarf, and
flames licked his face.

“Wake up!” yelled Lance’s mom.
“Cedric the Dragon has taken my
bracelet and scarf!”

Lance was brave.
"Cedric is a bad dragon," he said.
Lance raced after Cedric.

Lance walked into a cave. He saw Cedric and saw hot flames by Cedric's face.
"I do not like this place," said Lance.

"It is time for sleep," she tells her babies. "We might play again tonight."

SRA Early Interventions in Reading

The Opossum at Night

by Anne O'Brien
illustrated by Deborah Colvin Borgo

Columbus, OH

The McGraw-Hill Companies

SRAonline.com

SRA

Printed in the United States of America.

Send all inquiries to:
SRA/McGraw-Hill
8787 Orion Place
Columbus, OH 43240-4027

The McGraw-Hill Companies

The opossum returns to her tree.
Her babies are waiting.

107

Night is over. It begins to get light.

Mrs. Opossum does not like the light.
It is too bright. She sees better at night.

When it is night, she wakes.
She hunts for insects to feed her babies.

A dog frightens the opossum.
The opossum freezes. She stays still and plays dead.
She "plays opossum."

"No, we still make fudge cake by hand. It is not fast, but it is fun!"

Midge at the Farm

by Yve Knick
illustrated by Meryl Henderson

Columbus, OH

The McGraw-Hill Companies

SRAonline.com

SRA

Printed in the United States of America.

Send all inquiries to:
SRA/McGraw-Hill
8787 Orion Place
Columbus, OH 43240-4027

The McGraw·Hill Companies

"Can you help us with this fudge cake, Midge?" ask Gran and Gramps.

"Aren't there machines for that?" mumbles Midge.

"I can't help Gran and Gramps. This is not fun."

Farm Fun

"It is fun at Gran and Gramps's farm, Midge. When I was little, I helped them. Farm jobs are fun."

"I helped Gramps plant his garden, Midge. We chopped and tilled big patches of land. Then Gramps and I dropped in seeds."

"Gramps, can I help pick vegetables?"

"Vegetables are not picked by hand, Midge. This garden is just too big. Machines help pick vegetables. It is fast."

"Gran, can I help milk cows?"

"Cows are not milked by hand, Midge. Machines pump milk into big tubs. Then the milk gets pumped into jugs. It is fast."

"I helped Gran collect eggs, Midge. As hens scratched in pens, we picked eggs from hens' nests."

"I helped Gran milk her cows, Midge. Then at lunch, Gran, Gramps, and I sipped chilled milk in big, tall glasses. It was fun!"

"Gran, can I help collect eggs?"

"The eggs are not collected by hand, Midge. There are just too many hens. Machines collect the eggs. It is fast."

Fast Farm

“Gramps, can I help plant this garden?”

“The garden is not planted by hand, Midge. This garden is just too big. Machines chop and till and plant seeds. It is fast.”

“I helped Gramps pick vegetables, Midge. We’d rinse them and then munch and crunch them for snacks.”

“I helped Gran and Gramps make fudge cake with fresh eggs and milk that we collected. Mmmmm! It was such rich cake!”

“Just past that bridge is the farm! There are Gran and Gramps on the porch. They are glad to see us.”